Published in Louisville, Kentucky, by City on a Hill Studio.

Additional copies of this guide along with other *Manhood Journey* resources may be purchased online at **www.cityonahillstudio.com**.

LEADING LESSONS 1 ON 1 GUIDE

INTRODUCTION

Twitter is a goldmine for thought-provoking leadership quotes. Here are just a few:

> *"Your leadership effectiveness is never the result of one heroic act, it's always the sum of small faithful choices done every day." @danielsangi*

> *"God placed you on earth at this particular time in history. You live in a time of great challenges but enormous opportunity. #Leadership" @ExperiencingGod*

> *"You can either be comfortable or courageous today, but you can't be both." @ToddAdkins*

How do you define leadership? That's a big part of what this module is all about. Over the next six weeks you and your son will discuss what a leader is and does, but remember, dad, you are constantly modeling leadership for your son—and that modeling is, as the quote above relates, "the sum of small faithful choices done every day."

As a leader yourself—in your home, workplace, church, or wherever else you lead—be like the apostle Paul, who may have tweeted if it were possible at the time, "Follow my example, as I follow the example of Christ" (1 Cor. 11:1). Your model of godly leadership is Jesus. Follow him, abide in him, depend on him, and your son will follow in your footsteps.

WHO IS THIS GUIDE DESIGNED FOR? (AND WHAT IF I'M NOT THE BIOLOGICAL DAD?)

This Guide is designed for dads and their sons, but it's also for stepfathers, grandfathers, uncles, godfathers/guardians, coaches, teachers, small group leaders, or any other man who takes on the role of "dad" in a boy's life. (This Guide will use the terminology of "dad" and "son" to keep things simple.) Regardless of your title, thank you for stepping into this vital role in a young man's life. You have the incredible privilege of discipling this boy into a godly man. And, by the way, this Manhood Journey is for you, too! As you walk this trail together, you will discover and grow as an authentic man yourself.

If you are standing in as the father figure, the apostle Paul can be a good role model for you. He called Timothy, a young man he met on his missionary travels, his "true son in the faith" (1 Timothy 1:2). Look through 1 and 2 Timothy and watch for how Paul developed his son in the faith as a godly man and servant leader.

WHAT IF I'M USING THIS GUIDE WITH MORE THAN ONE BOY?

You can use this Guide with several boys at once, but it's designed to be used in a very small grouping of about two to four. One of the main purposes is to get to know your son(s) and have personal discussions with him. Manhood Journey also has studies for small groups of men and their sons, available at www.manhoodjourney.org.

CAN WE USE THIS GUIDE IF WE'RE NOT INVOLVED IN A MANHOOD JOURNEY SMALL GROUP?

Yes! While the small group program and the Guides work well together, you can meet with your son and use this guide separately from the group experience. Just skip any parts that refer directly to the group meetings (the "Group Session Review" section, for instance).

HOW CAN WE LEARN ABOUT, FIND, OR START A MANHOOD JOURNEY SMALL GROUP?

You can start or join an existing Manhood Journey small group with other men and their sons. Go to www.manhoodjourney.org to learn more, get started, or order your studies. The website even includes an interactive basic training for leaders.

The Manhood Journey small group program is a non-denominational, Bible-based approach to building young men through the discipleship and mentorship of fathers. It features guided Biblical discussion with hands-on, interactive activities. Groups consist of six to eight dads, who each bring their son(s). Young men without an engaged dad can be brought by a caring man who wants to pour into their life. Groups meet in six-week sprints at a church or someone's home with discussions guided by modules that cover various topics. The young men are normally between the ages of 8 and 17.

HOW DO I USE THIS GUIDE?

This guide is designed to provide you with ideas and a basic structure for spending time with and having meaningful conversations with your son. Some values that will help:

• Don't think of these sessions so much as "lesson plans," although you are in a position of "teacher" by being a good model for your son. Look at this book as a guide for you and your son to engage in discussions about godly manhood together.

• Each session purposely contains more content than you need. You know your son better than those who put this guide together. Use the ideas, discussions, and questions that best work for you and your son based on his age, personality, temperament, and understanding.

• Each session begins with "A Word to Dad" to help you think through the issues before you get together with your son. This opening page will encourage you in your vital role as a father.

• Each session is divided into four main sections:

1. BUILDING Our Relationship

A time for dad and son to review the group time and warm up for the day's topic. You'll begin your time with your son(s) by creating a "porch moment" together. Think of The Andy Griffith Show, when Andy and Opie would sit and chat on their front porch in Mayberry. Andy asked questions of his son and then listened well to his responses. They talked about what was going on in Opie's world, a world of schoolwork, sports, piano lessons, best friends, bullies, and girlfriends. Andy had a window into his son's world because of these times spent talking.

2. KNOWING God's Word

An opportunity to read, memorize, study, and apply the Bible to real, everyday life.

3. SERVING Others

This is the "so what" part. You will talk about how to put what you're learning into action to make an impact on others.

4. TALKING with God

You will close each time with your son with a brief time of prayer, simply talking with God about what you are learning and praying for your son(s).

YOU'LL NOTICE FIVE TYPES OF CONTENT IN THIS GUIDE:

1. Say: *This is material for you to read or paraphrase as you talk with your son. When possible, try to put these comments in your own words, but it's OK to read some of this brief content.*

2. Ask: *These are questions you will use to initiate discussion with your son(s). Be sure to listen to his response and ask your own follow-up questions to keep the conversation moving.*

3. Just for Dad—Instructions & Background Info: *These notes are included to help you lead these discussions with your son. They include some background material on Bible passages, ideas for you as you lead, and other helpful information. As the "Just for Dad" name implies, don't read this material out loud. You will do best in leading these sessions if you read through each one beforehand, and these instructions and background information will help.*

4. Just for Dad—Tips: *These are simple reminders and tips for you as you lead.*

5. Bible Passages: *Every session includes Scripture for you or your son to read. This is the foundation for these sessions!*

• *Have fun! Enjoy these valuable moments together with your son.*

FIVE VITAL PRINCIPLES
TO MAKE YOUR TIME WITH YOUR SON VALUABLE AND FRUITFUL

1. Take ownership of the process. In Ephesians 6:4, God's Word instructs fathers to bring up our children "in the training and instruction of the Lord." The Message translation says it even more directly: "Take them by the hand and lead them in the way of the Master." Dad, don't leave this to chance; bringing up sons to become godly men will not happen on its own. So initiate. Be strong and courageous. Be a man of action!

2. Be humble, honest, and helpful in all your conversations. The goal is authentic, godly manhood, so lead the way by being real, but only in ways that are beneficial to your son. Be prepared to share areas where you struggle in your faith and pursuit of being a godly man. Let your son see that you are a man who needs God's grace as you work toward godliness.

3. Engage in conversations, not lectures. Try not to give pat answers or solve your son's problems. Rather, talk out the issues and help him come to the answers on his own, with your guidance. Remember that more is caught than taught. If your son asks for your opinion, however, don't be afraid to give it as part of the discussion. Most importantly, take your questions to God, seeking wisdom from his Word. This Guide will help you do that.

4. Give attention to learning about your son. A major objective is to know his heart, which means you will need to unpeel numerous layers over the upcoming weeks. Ask questions. Use the discussion questions in this guide, but often the best discussions happen through the follow-up questions you ask that aren't in this guide. Then—and this critical!—listen. Listen not only to his words but also pay attention to his body language, tone of voice, and emotion. Here's another practical piece of advice: Put your cell phone or other electronic gadget away during your discussions. Let your son know he has your undivided attention while you meet together.

5. Apply biblical wisdom to real life. The Bible provides the answers to our questions. It is God's instruction book for our lives, and it is useful for teaching, rebuking, correcting, and training in righteousness (2 Tim. 3:16). Throughout these sessions, you will dig into the Scriptures as your primary source of wisdom.

HOW MUCH TIME WILL EACH SESSION TAKE?

The easy answer to this question is, "as long as it takes"! Time frames for each activity are purposely not included because one of the main goals of these Guides is to help you hang out with and talk with your son rather than work through a set, rigid agenda. These discussions can take approximately 45-60 minutes, but that time frame doesn't account for tossing ball, shooting baskets, and extended discussions. Try not to constantly look at your watch! If that might be a temptation, take it off and leave it on your nightstand.

You will be encouraged to build each session around activities your son and you enjoy. Take advantage of the time you have together to build memories as you build up your son.

WHAT OTHER SUPPLIES DO I NEED FOR THIS JOURNEY?

• *The most important thing you need as you embark on this journey is a willing heart, a desire for your son to become a godly man.*

• *Be sure to have a "Manhood Journey Notebook" for yourself and each son who is participating. You could buy a nice keepsake journal, or an inexpensive spiral bound version; but, make sure each person has something to write in. You will use these notebooks in these six sessions for note taking, illustrations, and more. Also, these notebooks will become like journals of your journey together. They will become keepsakes for both of you, like commemorative markers along the trail that will remind you in years to come of what God was doing in your life at this point in the journey.*

• *You and your son should each have your own Bible, whether it's a traditional printed Bible or a Bible app on your phone or other electronic device. Some shorter Scripture passages will be provided in this guide, but for most of the main passages, only references will be given. It's extremely valuable for you and your son to look these up in your Bibles.*

• *We have many other tools available for you. Find them on our website at **www.manhoodjourney.org**. There you'll find resources, blog posts, training, information about retreats, and much more.*

🐦 @manhoodjourney   📘 facebook.com/manhoodjourney

"So commit yourselves wholeheartedly to these words of mine. . . . Teach them to your children. Talk about them when you are at home and when you are on the road, when you are going to bed and when you are getting up." —Deuteronomy 11:18-19

DAD ... BEFORE YOU BEGIN

› *Read the Introduction. It includes very useful information for leading these times with your son.*

› *Be sure to have a "Manhood Journey Notebook" for yourself and each son who is participating. You could buy a nice keepsake journal, or an inexpensive spiral bound version; but, make sure each person has something to write in. You will use these in conjunction with the Dad's Guide, and they will become valuable keepsakes in the future!*

› *Write a note or letter to your son on the first page of his new Manhood Journey Notebook. Write this note before giving him his notebook or, if he already has it, borrow it from him. Write him a heartfelt note telling him what you're looking forward to during your journey together through Leading Lessons. Tell him specifically why you're proud of him and that you love him.*

LEADING LESSONS
WEEK 1

WHY LEADERS

MAKE RULES

A WORD TO DAD

Our heavenly Father is a God of justice and grace, truth and love, power and mercy. Some people like to focus on God's justice, so they talk about God's laws and his retribution for those who disobey. They view God as an all-powerful Judge. Others tend toward God's "softer" side; they describe him with words such as loving, merciful, forgiving, Daddy, and so forth.

Who's right? Both are. And yet, when either side ignores the other side of God's nature, they have a distorted image of God.

This is important! An accurate view of God's nature is foundational for living in a true relationship with him and for your own spiritual well-being. At the same time, realize that children develop their images of God from their earthly parents. As each of us matures in our relationship with God, we must look at God's Word to get a true picture of him and then sort out all of the distortions that we've accumulated over the years.

As you begin this Leading Lessons study with your son, you will have a wonderful opportunity to clarify who God is for both of you by looking at how the Bible describes him. God is still looking for leaders after his own heart (see 1 Sam. 13:14). For us to become those kinds of leaders, we must have a clear understanding of God's heart!

As you prepare for this time with your son, spend time with your heavenly Father, humbly asking him to help you to know him more, know his heart, and gain a biblically accurate awareness of him.

LEADING LESSONS
WEEK 1

BUILDING
OUR RELATIONSHIP

LEADING LESSONS 1 ON 1 GUIDE

GROUP SESSION REVIEW

Engage your son(s) in a dialogue about the meeting using any of the following questions:

• What did you learn about God during our meeting?

• What did you learn about the importance of rules and obedience?

• We read and discussed Leviticus 25:18, in which God said, "Follow my decrees (rules) and be careful to obey my laws, and you will live safely in the land." Why does God give us rules and laws?

• Why does God want us to obey the rules and laws he has given us?

• What does God promise to those who live his way rather than their own way?

• We talked about a foundational biblical leadership concept: A leader must enforce rules, but those rules should always be for the good of the followers as well as the leader. Why do you think that is important in a family, a group, a church, or any organization?

TIPS

IS THERE SUCH A THING AS A WRONG ANSWER?

Perhaps you've heard a motto for meetings, "There's no such thing as a wrong answer." That's actually a corruption of the axiom, "There's no such thing as a dumb question." There are wrong answers to your questions, especially when you are interpreting Scripture. The real question is how you handle a wrong answer from your son.

Handle correction with considerable care and wisdom! Here are a few thoughts:

• Be sure to not discourage your son by telling him he's wrong; instead, go straight to the source—God's Word rather than your own words—to get to the truth.

• Consider if you can let a somewhat wrong answer go for now, especially if it can be corrected later during your discussion about the Bible passages you'll be reading together.

• Ask yourself, How vital is it to correct this error? Is it a huge doctrinal issue or just a matter of personal opinion? Handle accordingly.

• If the truth is a biblically important one, utilize this tactic: First encourage your son for thinking through the issue at hand. Then say something such as, "Let's think more about this . . ." and then ask him more questions or look at the Bible to help him discover the truth. Then give him another word of encouragement for how he's thinking through the issue.

HOUSE RULES

Your Father/Son Homework this week is to discuss what rules you have in your household that are consistently disobeyed— by your son or any of your other children. Use the following questions to discuss the issues.

What rules for our household are consistently disobeyed?

You might start by talking in generalities about rules that "everyone" seems to ignore or disobey, but then move toward ones your son struggles to disobey. (This is not a time to chastise or scold; simply acknowledge what rules are ignored or disobeyed.)

Why do you think these rules are ignored or disobeyed (which is really the same thing!)? Is there a problem with these rules or something else?

Should the rules be changed or better enforced? Why?

LEADING LESSONS
WEEK 1

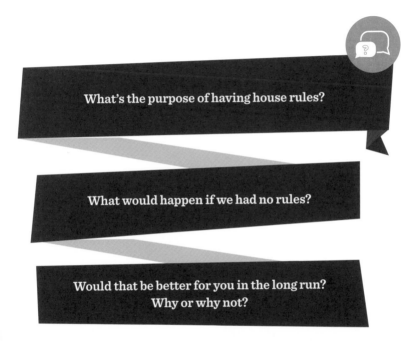

What's the purpose of having house rules?

What would happen if we had no rules?

Would that be better for you in the long run?
Why or why not?

KNOWING
GOD'S WORD

LEADING LESSONS 1 ON 1 GUIDE

This week you have two Bible verses to consider and memorize. With a younger son, memorize only the first verse. With a somewhat older son, memorize the second one. With an older, more mature young man, memorize both.

THEME VERSE

"If you love me, keep my commands."
John 14:15

"And this is love: that we walk in obedience to his commands. As you have heard from the beginning, his command is that you walk in love."
2 John 1:6

LEADING LESSONS
WEEK 1

Write both verses at the top of a new page in each of your Manhood Journey Notebooks.

Work together on memorizing the verse or verses.

Note that Jesus spoke the statement from John 14:15 as he met with his disciples the night before he was arrested, tried, and later crucified. In the passage from 2 John 1, the apostle John was telling his audience (including us) that we are to love one another. In this verse he described what real love is.

What do these two verses have in common?

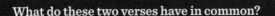

Both equate love with obeying Jesus.

In what ways is obeying someone a form of loving them?

You might point out that love is not just an emotion or a feeling; it's a decision of the will, an action.

SAY

God's commands are not for his benefit, but for ours and for his kingdom. Just as we need rules in our household so that life is better for everyone in the family, God has established rules for us so that our lives may go well for us, so that we may live an abundant life. God is our Creator, so he knows what's best for us and what will harm us. God's commands are not random; he didn't make them up just to annoy us or take away our freedom. He gave them to us because he loves us and wants us to live a full life just as he created us to live. If we trust God and do what he tells us to do, we can live a much better, more joyful, and more productive life.

Let's dig deeper into some of the commands Jesus gave us for living a full, joy-filled life.

LEADING LESSONS
WEEK 1

DIGGING DEEPER

SAY

As Jesus met people who needed healing, he sometimes gave them a command to follow in relation to making them well:

• Jesus told a man with a deformed hand to stand in front of everybody and then stretch out his hand (Mk. 3:1-5).

• He commanded a paralyzed man, "Stand up, pick up your mat, and go home" (Matt. 9:6).

• He charged ten lepers to "go show yourselves to the priests" (Lk. 17:14).

• He directed a blind man to "go wash yourself in the pool of Siloam" (John 9:7).

What might have happened if the people who needed Jesus' healing refused to do what he told them to do?

LEADING LESSONS
WEEK 1

What can we learn from the people Jesus healed about how to respond to Jesus when he gives us a command?

We should understand that Jesus wants the best for us, but we need to do things his way in order to receive his blessings in our lives. We should listen to him and obey him because we know he is powerful and has the ability to heal us and give us life to the full.

Read Matthew 22:34-40 in your own Bibles.

What did Jesus say are the greatest commands?

Why are those the greatest commands?

When we obey the commands to love God and one another, all of the other commands become natural to us.

LEADING LESSONS
WEEK 1

**Read Matthew 28:16-20
in your own Bibles.**

What did Jesus command his followers to do?

It began with something very basic, to go to the mountain where Jesus told them to go (v. 16). He also told them—and us—to:

*• **Go:** not stay where they were, but to get out of their comfort zones and go where hurting, lost people were (v. 19)*

*• **Make disciples:** introduce more people to Jesus and invite them to follow him (v. 19)*

*• **Baptize:** Immerse them in water into a changed life (v. 19)*

*• **Teach:** instruct them to do what Jesus taught them to do—obey Jesus' commands (v. 20)*

**LEADING LESSONS
WEEK 1**

SAY

I want you to notice one more important part of this Scripture passage. In verse 18, Jesus reminded his followers that the Father had given him all authority in heaven and earth. We'll talk more about this in week 3, but it's important now to mention that we obey God as well as human leaders because they have authority.

Jesus had authority because he was the Son of God. His Father in heaven gave him that authority. Au-thority is always given to us by someone else. We don't just take it or assume it. I have authority as your dad because God gave me that authority in the Bible (i.e., Eph. 6:1-4).

EVEN DEEPER

If you would like to dig even deeper into what the Bible says about the importance of rules and obedience, look up and discuss the following Scripture passages. (Write these references in your Manhood Journey Notebooks.)

2 Kings 5:1-14
Matthew 8:5-14
John 14:23-24
John 15:9-17
Romans 13:8-10

SERVING
OTHERS

LEADING LESSONS 1 ON 1 GUIDE

LEADING LESSONS
WEEK 1

SAY

Like King David, I want to be a leader who is a man after God's heart. I also want you to become a godly leader—right now in your school and among your friends and in the future in your family, workplace, church, or wherever else God places you.

Our best model for godly leadership is Jesus. As we saw in our study, Jesus was given authority to lead, so he led with boldness and confidence. He provided his followers with commands and told them ahead of time how important it was for them, and for God's kingdom, that they obey him. Jesus' commands for his followers are for our benefit, to help us live as godly leaders in our circles of influence.

Our greatest commands are to love God with all our hearts, souls, and minds, and to love others. When we love God and others, we'll naturally do what Jesus told us to do: to go and help other people follow him.

LEADING LESSONS
WEEK 1

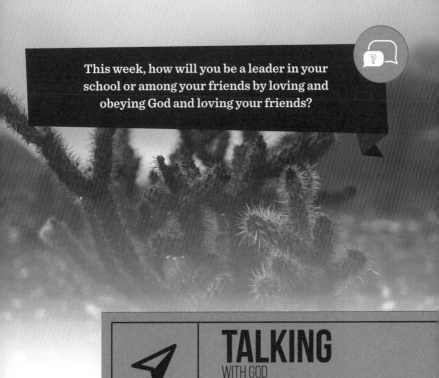

This week, how will you be a leader in your school or among your friends by loving and obeying God and loving your friends?

TALKING
WITH GOD

LEADING LESSONS 1 ON 1 GUIDE

Spend time with your son praying together for your family, people you work with, his friends at school or in the neighborhood, and anyone else God has placed in your lives. Use any of the following prompts as needed:

LEADING LESSONS
WEEK 1

SAY

• Father, all authority in heaven and earth is yours. You are our King Eternal, our Creator, our Lord, and our Master.

• Thank you for giving us opportunities to make a difference for you in the lives of people you put around us.

• Thank you for the authority you give to us as leaders here on earth. Remind us that this authority is not our own, but it comes from you and is for you.

• Thank you, Lord, for the rules and commands you've given us to guide our lives so that we can live this life to the full for you and for your glory.

• Give us wisdom and strength to live in obedience to you.

• Help us to be leaders who are more and more like Jesus. We want our lives to honor you and bring you glory.

LEADING LESSONS
WEEK 2

LEADERS

FOLLOW FIRST

A WORD TO DAD

Jesus started his church by calling a few normal, workaday guys to follow him, and then he made a remarkable statement. He told these unschooled fishermen he'd make them into fishers of men (Matt. 4:18-20). What did Jesus mean by fishers of men? He was telling them he'd turn them into men who would make an eternal difference in people's lives; he'd make them leaders.

Jesus reiterated the point sometime later when he called together a bunch of the folks he had asked to follow him and asked 12 of them to take their following to the next level. He asked these disciples to be a part of a select small group of "apostles," men who would be sent out to lead (Mark 6:13).

That's what Jesus does, still, today. He takes regular, ordinary men and women and calls them; first as followers and then as sent leaders. It's always in that order. A man who cannot be a humble follower should never become a leader.

By following the Master Leader, you learn how to lead and how not to lead. As you spend time with him, you see his heart for people and you catch hold of that great compassion. As you abide with him, he pours his love and power and grace into you so that you can then overflow that same love, power, and grace into those around you. In other words, following Jesus makes you into a leader.

The birthplace of any real Christian leader is a follower of Jesus who becomes more and more like Him.

LEADING LESSONS
WEEK 2

Before you lead your son through this time together, first be sure to be a follower. Spend time with Jesus and allow him to saturate your mind and heart with his love and wisdom. Don't pray—at least not in the way you usually think of prayer, as uttering so many words. Just sit with Jesus and enjoy his presence. Ask him to lead you. Then let him.

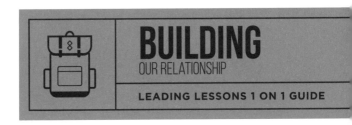

BUILDING
OUR RELATIONSHIP

LEADING LESSONS 1 ON 1 GUIDE

GROUP SESSION REVIEW

Engage your son(s) in a dialogue about the meeting using any of the following questions:

From what you learned in our group discussion and activities, why do we need leaders?

LEADING LESSONS
WEEK 2

SAY

We looked at 1 Samuel 8:4-5, when the people asked Samuel to appoint a king to lead them, because all the other nations around them had kings.

What was wrong with their request?

The fact that everyone else is doing it is not a good reason for anything! God was the Israelites' King and the people were not even following him; they had rejected him as their King (vv. 7-8). They were using human reasoning rather than listening to and following God.

Does that mean that having human leaders is wrong?

No. The Israelites had had other kinds of leaders, such as Moses, Joshua, the judges, and Samuel, for instance. People need human leaders who follow God and lead out of their own relationship with him. The Israelites, however, wanted a human leader/king who would "lead us and go out before us and fight our battles" (v. 20). That was God's job!

LEADING LESSONS
WEEK 2

In our meeting, we played the "follow the leader" guessing game, where someone had to guess who was leading the group. What did you learn from that activity?

What's more important, to be a good follower or a good leader? Why?

What are some of the qualities of a good follower?

What do good followers do?

In the discussion, we talked about three things: (1) they sacrifice their own wants and needs; (2) they don't seek instant gratification and short-term benefits; and (3) they don't believe their leaders are infallible heroes.

LEADING LESSONS
WEEK 2

ROLE MODELS

Discuss who your role-model leaders were when you were growing up and who they are now. Tell your son why you looked up to these leaders.

Who are some of your leadership role models?

Why did you select them?
What leadership qualities do you see in them?

How do you think they became leaders?
What did they do to become leaders?
What practices do you think they made a part of their routines?
Who did they model themselves after?

LEADING LESSONS
WEEK 2

If you looked only to them for your definition of what a leader is, what words would you use to describe leadership?

KNOWING
GOD'S WORD

LEADING LESSONS 1 ON 1 GUIDE

THEME VERSE

"Follow my example, as I follow the example of Christ."
1 Corinthians 11:1

LEADING LESSONS
WEEK 2

Write this verse at the top of a new page in each of your Manhood Journey Notebooks.

This verse should be an easy one for both of you to memorize, but that doesn't make it any less vital! Spend time saying it aloud and discussing its meaning and implications for you.

SAY

The apostle Paul was telling the people he loved in the city of Corinth the same thing I want to say to you. I want to be a godly man who follows Christ Jesus in my life, and as I follow the example of how Jesus lived, I want you to follow my example.

This verse is only 10 words long, yet it gives us such a great picture of what Christian leadership is all about. Christian leaders are first of all followers of Jesus. Then they invite others to follow them as they follow Christ.

Let's dig a little deeper into the context of what Paul was saying here.

DIGGING DEEPER

**Read or ask your son to read
1 Corinthians 10:31—11:3.**

"Whether you eat or drink or whatever you do, do it all for the glory of God. Do not cause anyone to stumble, whether Jews, Greeks or the church of God—even as I try to please everyone in every way. For I am not seeking my own good but the good of many, so that they may be saved. Follow my example, as I follow the example of Christ. I praise you for remembering me in everything and for holding to the traditions just as I passed them on to you. But I want you to realize that the head of every man is Christ."

In what ways was Paul a model of living the Christian life for the Corinthians?

LEADING LESSONS
WEEK 2

SAY

In Philippians 2, Paul talked about how we should all seek to be like Christ: "Do nothing out of selfish ambition or vain conceit. Rather, in humility value others above yourselves, not looking to your own interests but each of you to the interests of the others" (vv. 3-4).

Look back at the 1 Corinthians passage, especially 10:34. How did Paul follow the example of Jesus?

Like Christ, Paul looked to the interests of others above his own interests. This takes humility and self-sacrifice.

Why is it important for a Christian leader to realize that the head of every person is Christ?

Christ Jesus is the head of the church, that is, the body of Christ (see Eph. 4:15; 5:23; Col. 1:18; 2:19). He is ultimately the leader of the church, so we lead under his authority and to carry out his mission, not our own!

LEADING LESSONS
WEEK 2

SAY

Let's look at a few specific ways that we can learn how to lead as we follow Jesus.

Write the following table in each of your Manhood Journey Notebooks. Read each verse and then write what you see as the leadership qualities of Jesus.

Verse	Leadership Quality of Jesus
Matthew 9:35	
Matthew 11:29	
Matthew 16:24	
John 8:28b-29	
John 10:14	

LEADING LESSONS
WEEK 2

What other leadership qualities of Jesus have you noticed as you've read the Bible?

EVEN DEEPER

If you would like to dig even deeper into what the Bible says about being a Christ follower before becoming a Christian leader, look up and discuss the following Scripture passages. (Write these references in your Manhood Journey Notebooks.)

1 Peter 2:21
1 Corinthians 4:14-17
Romans 15:1-3
Matthew 4:18-20
John 17:18

LEADING LESSONS
WEEK 2

SERVING
OTHERS

LEADING LESSONS 1 ON 1 GUIDE

To become a good leader, you must first become an authentic follower of Jesus. What areas of following Jesus can you strengthen?

Everyone can work at growing in our relationship with Jesus by abiding more with him, reading his word, growing bolder in prayer, and so forth.

Which of the leadership qualities of Jesus that we discussed do you need to improve at?

How will you work on those?

LEADING LESSONS
WEEK 2

To whom could you say, "Follow my example as I follow the example of Christ"?

This may be a younger sibling, a friend or classmate, or someone else. Be sure to share who in your circles of influence you hope to lead toward Christ by your actions and words.

TALKING
WITH GOD

LEADING LESSONS 1 ON 1 GUIDE

Spend time together lifting up praises and prayers to God. Use any of the following to help prompt your conversation with God:

SAY

• Lord, as we read in 1 Corinthians 10:31, we desire to do everything we do—everything we do—for your glory.

• Help us to continually become men who seek

to bring you, not ourselves, glory in the way we live every minute of every day, as we work or study or play or have conversations with friends or relax—even as we sleep.

• Father, we also seek to be followers of you. We want to follow your Son Jesus and to be led by your Holy Spirit.

• Lord, give me wisdom and power as I seek to be a godly example for others to follow. Help me be a model of your love, compassion, and servant leadership.

• Lord Jesus, you are our Savior and King. You willingly went to the cross and took our sins upon yourself so that we may be forgiven and be reconciled with the Father. But death could not win the victory over you; you rose from the dead and have given us hope for everlasting life in heaven! You taught us the ultimate lesson of sacrificial leadership.

• We praise you, Jesus, not only with our words but with our lives as we seek to bring glory to you!

LEADING LESSONS
WEEK 3

POWER:
THE FIRST "P" OF LEADERSHIP

A WORD TO DAD

The President of the United States is one of the most powerful and influential leaders in the world. What can you learn from these leaders? Look at these four presidential quotes. What do they have in common? What do they teach you about authentic leadership?

> *"Nearly all men can stand adversity, but if you want to test a man's character, give him power."*
> **–President Abraham Lincoln**

> *"People ask the difference between a leader and a boss. The leader leads, and the boss drives."*
> **–President Theodore Roosevelt**

> *"You do not lead by hitting people over the head. That's assault, not leadership."*
> **–President Dwight D. Eisenhower**

> *"The greatest leader is not necessarily the one who does the greatest things. He is the one that gets the people to do the greatest things."*
> **–President Ronald Reagan**

Take a moment and answer these questions in your Manhood Journey Notebook: (1) What attributes of real leadership do you see? (2) What myths about leadership do these quotes address? (3) What place does power have in leadership?

LEADING LESSONS
WEEK 3

Last week, you and your son discussed the idea that a great leader must first be a follower. This week you'll talk about the fact that leaders who want to lead powerfully must first become weak, meek, or humble.

The most powerful leader ever was not a president, but a humble servant. He said, "The greatest among you should be like the youngest, and the one who rules like the one who serves" (Luke 22:26). As you lead, seek to be more like him.

BUILDING
OUR RELATIONSHIP

LEADING LESSONS 1 ON 1 GUIDE

GROUP SESSION REVIEW

Engage your son(s) in a dialogue about the meeting using any of the following questions:

LEADING LESSONS
WEEK 3

• What words would you use to define leadership?

• What are the differences between how the world defines "power" for a leader and the way the Bible defines it?

• In our meeting, we discussed two ways Jesus developed his power as a leader: (1) He was an expert in his area and (2) he served humbly. What did you learn about leadership from these two "power tips"?

• What does it look like to be a humble leader?

• In what ways is humility powerful for a godly leader?

• At the beginning of our meeting, we talked about several quotations about leadership. Here's one more. Benjamin Hooks said, "If you think you are leading and turn around to see no one following, then you are just taking a walk." Do you agree or disagree? Why?

WEAK DAYS

Discuss with your son the times in your life when you've felt weak. (For example, did you get beaten up or otherwise bullied by bigger kids, try to lift weights but didn't start out very strong, perform poorly at a tryout and get cut, or get sick a lot?) The point is to admit weaknesses so your son sees you in a more humble way.

**LEADING LESSONS
WEEK 3**

What is a time when you've felt
weak rather than strong?

What did you do about it?

KNOWING
GOD'S WORD

LEADING LESSONS 1 ON 1 GUIDE

*THEME
VERSE* "Anyone who wants to be
first must be the very last,
and the servant of all."
Mark 9:35

LEADING LESSONS
WEEK 3

Write this verse at the top of a new page in each of your Manhood Journey Notebooks.

Work together on memorizing the verse.

SAY

Jesus said this to his disciples after they had been arguing with each other about which one of them in the group was the greatest. Remember that Jesus was training his followers to become leaders, so this was an important lesson for them!

What was the problem with the disciples that Jesus needed to deal with?

They were putting themselves rather than others first. They were arrogant. They thought of leadership as power and greatness rather than being a servant.

LEADING LESSONS
WEEK 3

What was Jesus teaching them about leadership?

Leaders are humble servants.

DIGGING DEEPER

SAY

Jesus taught his disciples about servant leadership but he also modeled it for them. He said, "For even the Son of Man did not come to be served, but to serve" (Mk. 10:45). Jesus turned the world's ideas of leadership upside-down. The world taught, and still teaches, that leadership is all about human power, influence, and intelligence. In Jesus' day, kings and even religious leaders expected to be served by their subjects. "Not so with you," Jesus said. "Instead, whoever wants to become great among you must be your servant" (Mk. 10:43).

LEADING LESSONS WEEK 3

Can you think of an example of when you led someone by serving them? What happened?

This is a great opportunity, dad, to share examples of how you seek to lead your family or at your workplace by serving.

SAY

Serving others takes humility as we put other people above ourselves. Leadership does still involve power, but not the kind of power the world relies on. In the world, power means you get to boss other people around, you get the biggest and best office, and you make the most money. According to the world, power in leadership means you have authority over them.

For followers of Christ, God has ultimate authority. He is all powerful, so whatever power we have comes from him. That's why the apostle Paul said, "I can do everything through Christ, who gives me strength" (Phil. 4:13, NLT).

So, Christian leaders lead under the authority of Christ, who gives us the power and strength we need to lead well.

LEADING LESSONS
WEEK 3

Draw the following illustration of godly leadership in your Manhood Journey Notebook. Have your son draw it in his notebook as well.

JESUS AUTHORITY

HIS POWER

OUR LEADERSHIP

SERVING

PEOPLE WE LEAD

SAY

As we read the Gospels, we see Jesus teach and train his disciples to be leaders, and he modeled what godly leadership looked like for them. Jesus constantly told them that his authority came from his heavenly Father (see John 3:35; 5:27, 30; 7:28-29:10; 17:2; Eph. 1:18-23; Phil. 2:9-10). But then Jesus gave his disciples some of that authority to minister and to lead (see Matt. 10:1; 2 Cor. 13:10; 1 Thess. 4:2). Today, Jesus gives us that same kind of authority. And with that authority comes his power!

Let's look at a couple examples of this in our Bibles.

Read or ask your son to read Matthew 28:16-20.

LEADING LESSONS
WEEK 3

SAY

In this lesson, we're studying the first "P" of leadership: Power. And remember that power comes with authority (refer to illustration you drew in your Manhood Journey Notebooks).

What leadership power did Jesus give to this disciples?

The authority and power to make disciples, to baptize them into Christ, and to teach.

Why do you think this passage begins with the disciples worshiping Jesus?

There are a lot of right answers here. Jesus had risen from the dead. They knew Jesus was the Son of God, the Messiah. Having an attitude of worship always comes before serving and leading. Worship puts God in his rightful place and us in ours, which is necessary to receive his power.

Let's talk about three more "P" words that we see in this passage. They are: (1) Jesus' Presence, (2) Jesus' Promises, and (3) Jesus' Purposes.

*On a new page in your Manhood Journey Notebooks, write these
four "P" words. Leave space between each one to write notes as
you discuss these.*

Jesus' POWER

Jesus' PROMISES

Jesus' PRESENCE

Jesus' PURPOSES

**What promises do you see in this passage,
Matthew 28:16-20?**

*There are several good answers, but move toward the end
of verse 20: "Surely I am with you always, to the very end
of the age."*

Jesus' Promise leads to his Presence. He is with
us. Earlier, he had told his disciples that whenever
even two or three of them met together in his
name, he'd be there with them (Matt. 18:20). So,
we must realize that as we meet together to
become more godly men, Jesus is literally here
with us. He is present right now! His power is
available to us. He is working to bring about his
promises in and through us!

**LEADING LESSONS
WEEK 3**

If Jesus is with us, what kind of Power do we have to minister and to lead?

Jesus' power is unlimited! Even the power of superheroes has some limitations, but not Jesus'! That means that we can do everything, as long as it is according to his purposes, through Christ who gives us strength!

What are Jesus' Purposes for us?

See verses 19-20: to make disciples, baptize them into Christ, and teach (disciple) them how to live for Jesus.

SAY

To lead with Jesus' POWER, we must also understand his PROMISES, recognize his PRESENCE with us, and lead according to his (not our own) PURPOSES.

LEADING LESSONS
WEEK 3

EVEN DEEPER

If you would like to dig even deeper into what the Bible says about leading with Jesus' power and authority, look up and discuss the following Scripture passages. (Write these references in your Manhood Journey Notebooks.)

Acts 1:6-8
Deuteronomy 31:6-8
Acts 18:9-11
Luke 10:17-22
Jude 24-25

LEADING LESSONS
WEEK 3

SERVING
OTHERS

LEADING LESSONS 1 ON 1 GUIDE

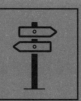

SAY

Let's discuss how specifically we can lead with Jesus' power this week. Think of a situation that may come up this week in which you can take a leadership role.

What's the situation?

What PROMISES from God do you want to trust in as you seek to serve and lead?

LEADING LESSONS
WEEK 3

In what specific ways will Jesus' PRESENCE with you give you what you need to lead well?

What PURPOSES of God will you be fulfilling as you lead?

TALKING
WITH GOD

LEADING LESSONS 1 ON 1 GUIDE

SAY

As we'll discuss in Week 5, PRAYER is another vital "P" word when it comes to leading with Jesus' power. So let's close out our time together in prayer.

Use any of the following prayer prompts as you see fit:

LEADING LESSONS
WEEK 3

• Jesus, we do recognize that you really are present with us as we meet. Thank you for being here with us and for never leaving us nor forsaking us!

• Father, thank you for providing us with the authority and power we need to serve others and to lead well. We don't lead on our own, but we only do what you direct us to do.

• We lead under your authority. We don't want to say anything or teach anything or do anything except for what comes from you. You are our Lord, our Leader, our Master, our King.

• We pray that out of your glorious riches you may strengthen us with POWER through your Spirit in our inner beings, so that Christ may dwell in our hearts through faith. And we pray that we, being rooted and established in your love, may have POWER, together with all your holy people, to grasp how wide and long and high and deep is the love of Christ, and to know this love that surpasses knowledge—that we may be filled to the measure of all your fullness. Now to you, Lord, who are able to do immeasurably more than all we ask or imagine, according to your POWER that is at work within us, to you be glory in the church and in your son Christ Jesus throughout all generations, for ever and ever! Amen (adapted from Ephesians 3:16-21).

LEADING LESSONS
WEEK 4

PROVERBS:
THE SECOND "P" OF LEADERSHIP

A WORD TO DAD

The book of Proverbs was written about 30 centuries ago, yet its wisdom is still as relevant as ever. Many of these proverbs express a contrast. For instance, "A wise son brings joy to his father, but a foolish son brings grief to his mother" (10:1). Many proverbs describe rewards or consequences for certain behaviors. For example, "The righteous man walks in his integrity; His children are blessed after him" (20:7, NKJV), and "Stern discipline awaits anyone who leaves the path; the one who hates correction will die" (15:10).

Solomon wrote many but not all of these proverbs. He stated his general purpose up front:

> *Their purpose is to teach people wisdom and discipline, to help them understand the insights of the wise. Their purpose is to teach people to live disciplined and successful lives, to help them do what is right, just, and fair. These proverbs will give insight to the simple, knowledge and discernment to the young (1:2-4, NLT).*

Like you, Solomon often spoke as a mentor to his son: "Listen, my son, to your father's instruction and do not forsake your mother's teaching" (1:8). But there are many bits of wisdom for you as a dad as well: "The father of a righteous son will rejoice greatly, and one who fathers a wise son will delight in him" (23:24, HCSB).

If you want to be a leader of any type—in your home, at work, in your church or community—Proverbs is a must-read. These are godly principles for living life to the full. The idea is that you

LEADING LESSONS
WEEK 4

internalize these biblical values and principles in your own life and then pass them on to your son . . . just as David passed them on to Solomon, who did the same with his sons.

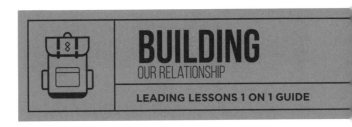

BUILDING
OUR RELATIONSHIP

LEADING LESSONS 1 ON 1 GUIDE

GROUP SESSION REVIEW

Engage your son(s) in a dialogue about the meeting using any of the following questions.

- What did you learn about the book of Proverbs?
- What is the purpose of this Bible book?
- What can we gain from reading it?
- How can Proverbs help us be more godly leaders?

LEADING LESSONS
WEEK 4

WORDS OF WISDOM

> How would most of your friends define wisdom?

> How about you? Is your definition of wisdom any different from theirs? If so, what is it?

SAY

Let's look at a few dictionary definitions of wisdom.
Merriam-Webster defines wisdom as:

**LEADING LESSONS
WEEK 4**

SAY

•knowledge that is gained by having many experiences in life

• the natural ability to understand things that most other people cannot understand

•knowledge of what is proper or reasonable: good sense or judgment

The Oxford English Dictionary defines it as, "the quality of having experience, knowledge, and good judgment."

Dictionary.com defines it like this: "knowledge of what is true or right coupled with just judgment as to action; sagacity, discernment, or insight."

Which of those sound like the best definition of wisdom to you?

LEADING LESSONS
WEEK 4

SAY

Now let's see how the Bible defines wisdom:

"Understanding what is really important in life. This wisdom comes from God" (New Century Bible Dictionary).

"Knowledge, understanding, applying knowledge and insights to life situations. Wisdom in the Bible usually refers to a God-given ability, rather than human common sense" (What the Bible is All About).

From these definitions, what is the difference between wisdom and knowledge?

Knowledge is the grasping of factual information, but knowing the facts isn't enough. We must know how to use the facts! That's where wisdom comes in. For example, some people know about God, but that's not enough. A wise person really knows God and follows him. Wisdom is more than knowing; it puts what we know into action.

**LEADING LESSONS
WEEK 4**

KNOWING
GOD'S WORD

LEADING LESSONS 1 ON 1 GUIDE

"The wisdom that comes from heaven is first of all pure; then peace-loving, considerate, submissive, full of mercy and good fruit, impartial and sincere."
James 3:17

THEME VERSE

Write this verse at the top of a new page in each of your Manhood Journey Notebooks.

Work together on memorizing this verse. It might help to list each of the attributes of wisdom listed in the verse in a vertical list in your Manhood Journey Notebooks under the verse itself. Talk about what each of these attributes means, if your son isn't sure.

LEADING LESSONS
WEEK 4

From where does wisdom come?

James 3:17 says, "heaven." You might also have your son look up Proverbs 2:6, which says that the Lord gives wisdom.

DIGGING DEEPER

SAY

Solomon wrote much of Proverbs. But from where did he get all his wisdom? The Bible tells us the story.

Read 1 Kings 3:5-15.

LEADING LESSONS WEEK 4

Why do you think Solomon asked for wisdom?

It's intriguing that Solomon had enough wisdom to ask for wisdom!

What was God's response to Solomon's request?

The obvious answer is that God gave him wisdom, but move beyond that. Follow up with, "How did God feel about Solomon and his request?" "What else did God give Solomon, and why?"

Solomon was the king of Israel as his father, David, before him was. How do you think wisdom would help him be a good leader?

LEADING LESSONS
WEEK 4

Choose a chapter from Proverbs to read and study together. Some suggestions: Proverbs 3; 10; 16; 19; 21; 27.

Ask these questions for whatever passage you choose:

Which proverb (verse) stands out to you the most?

Why did you choose that one?

What does it say to you?

How can you live by that?

LEADING LESSONS **WEEK 4**

Dad, choose your own favorite verse as well. Write both of your verses in your Manhood Journey Notebooks, labeling each with your names and the date. These may be good verses for you to memorize and discuss in the future.

Are there any verses you don't like? Which one?

Why do you dislike it?

Why did God put it in the Bible?

LEADING LESSONS
WEEK 4

What other wisdom do you gain from this chapter of Proverbs?

How would it benefit your life to read through Proverbs once a year?

How would reading Proverbs help you to be a wise leader?

There was another leader who was even wiser than Solomon. He was one of Solomon's descendants. Can you guess who it is?

Hint: Much of the New Testament is about him. He also got his wisdom from God—directly from God. He was God's Son. He's Jesus!

LEADING LESSONS
WEEK 4

SAY

The gospel writer Luke described Jesus as a boy: "And the child grew and became strong; he was filled with wisdom, and the grace of God was on him" (2:40). Jesus was filled with wisdom even as a young boy, but he continued to grow in wisdom (see v. 52) as he became older.

What will you do to continue to grow in wisdom in your life?

One thing you and your son can do is to stay in God's Word, which contains wisdom for living life to the full. You can read the book of Proverbs once a year. You can be sure you are friends with wise people, not fools.

**LEADING LESSONS
WEEK 4**

EVEN DEEPER

If you would like to dig even deeper into what the Bible says about wisdom, look up and discuss the following Scripture passages. (Write these references in your Manhood Journey Notebooks.)

1 Kings 3:16-28
1 Kings 4:29-34
Ecclesiastes 9:13-18
Matthew 7:24-29
1 Corinthians 2:6-9

SERVING
OTHERS

LEADING LESSONS 1 ON 1 GUIDE

How do we demonstrate that we have wisdom?

We don't have to prove it to anyone and we don't proudly flaunt our wisdom. Yet, people can tell we have wisdom by the way we live.

Read James 3:13.

*"Who is wise and understanding among you?
Let them show it by their good life, by deeds
done in the humility that comes from wisdom."*

Write this verse in your Manhood Journey Notebooks.

What words describe a person who is wise?

*Circle these words in your notebooks. Possibilities include
"good life," "deeds," and "humility."*

**LEADING LESSONS
WEEK 4**

Why are these attributes of wisdom?

As you continue to grow as a wise leader this week, what good deeds will you do in humility for others?

TALKING
WITH GOD

LEADING LESSONS 1 ON 1 GUIDE

Before spending time in prayer with your son, read James 1:5:

"If any of you lacks wisdom, you should ask God, who gives generously to all without finding fault, and it will be given to you."

Use any of these prompts to lead your prayer time.

LEADING LESSONS
WEEK 4

SAY

• O God, we worship you as our Creator, Savior, and the Leader of our lives. You are all-powerful, all knowing, and all wise.

• We confess that we have failed to live in your ways and to give you the glory you deserve.

• Thank you, Father, for your forgiveness.

• As Solomon did, we ask you to give us wisdom.

• Give us a discerning heart to lead wisely and to distinguish right from wrong.

• As we grow in wisdom, Lord, we ask that our wisdom be pure, peace-loving, considerate, submissive, full of mercy and good fruit, impartial, and sincere.

• Thank you for helping us grow in strength and wisdom. Thank you for your love. Thank you for giving us life to the full, and thank you for giving us eternal life through your Son, Jesus.

LEADING LESSONS
WEEK 5

PRAYER:
THE THIRD "P" OF LEADERSHIP

A WORD TO DAD

It is impossible to become a godly man, much less a godly leader, without prayer.

Manhood Journey is about becoming godly men who can then be a positive influence on the world around us. Prayer is an indispensable, foundational part of this journey. It, along with Scripture, imparts the wisdom we need along the journey. Prayer supplies the strength we need as we climb these rugged trails together. It often provides the direction we need to stay on the right path. It keeps us connected to the One who has blazed these trails and knows them best.

One of the most important things you can do as a leader of your family is to pray each day for your wife and children. Pray also for your extended family, co-workers, neighbors, kids' friends, and anyone else in your spheres of influence. But don't forget to pray for yourself as well. Prayer is about spending time with God, communicating with him, drawing closer to him, worshiping him, thanking him, confessing to him, and asking him for what you need.

> **Ask and it will be given to you; seek and you will find; knock and the door will be opened to you. For everyone who asks receives; the one who seeks finds; and to the one who knocks, the door will be opened. "Which of you, if your son asks for bread, will give him a stone? Or if he asks for a fish, will give him a snake? If you, then, though you are evil, know how to give good gifts to your children, how much more will your Father in heaven give good gifts to those who ask him! (Matthew 7:7-11).**

LEADING LESSONS
WEEK 5

LEADING LESSONS 1 ON 1 GUIDE

GROUP SESSION REVIEW

Engage your son(s) in a dialogue about the meeting using any of the following questions:

- **What did you think of the meeting overall?**

- **What did you learn from the "magic" Danish Elephant activity at the beginning of the meeting?**

- **What are some things we can do to allow God to saturate our minds?**

- **In what ways is prayer an "adventure with God"? (See Jeremiah 33:3.)**

- **What did you learn about how to pray from the Lord's Prayer?**

LEADING LESSONS
WEEK 5

SAY

Let's pray the Lord's Model Prayer together before we move into the rest of our time together.

Our Father in heaven,
hallowed be your name,
your kingdom come,
your will be done,
on earth as it is in heaven.
Give us today our daily bread.
And forgive us our debts,
as we also have forgiven our debtors.
And lead us not into temptation,
but deliver us from the evil one.
                                    -Matthew 6:9-13

TIPS

Pray this model for prayer now with your son, emphasizing that this is a model for prayer. Jesus began by telling his followers, "This, then, is how [not what] you should pray" (v. 9, emphasis and explanation added). Also lead your whole family through this model prayer sometime this week.

LEADING LESSONS
WEEK 5

OLD CAMEL KNEES

Listen closely to the following statement:

An effective leader is a fervent prayer.
Do you agree or disagree with that? Why?

SAY

Last week we talked about the importance of wisdom in being a godly leader, but it's impossible to gain wisdom without prayer. Remember how we ended our time together in prayer last week. We looked at James 1:5, which says, "If any of you lacks wisdom, you should ask God." Throughout his letter, James discussed the vitality of prayer in a Christian's life. We'll look at a few of those verses today.

According to church tradition, James was known as "Old Camel Knees," because he had built up thick callouses on his knees from hours spent on them praying to God. It makes sense that James would be known as a prayer warrior. After all, his brother, Jesus, was also a great man of prayer. We'll also look at how prayer made Jesus a great leader.

How would you feel if people called you "Old Camel Knees"?

In what ways would you consider that a compliment?

KNOWING
GOD'S WORD

LEADING LESSONS 1 ON 1 GUIDE

THEME VERSE "The prayer of a righteous person is powerful and effective."
James 5:16b

LEADING LESSONS
WEEK 5

Write this verse at the top of a new page in each of your Manhood Journey Notebooks.

Work together to memorize this verse. For young men who want a bigger challenge, memorize the entire verse:

Therefore confess your sins to each other and pray for each other so that you may be healed. The prayer of a righteous person is powerful and effective (James 5:16).

DIGGING DEEPER

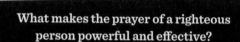

What makes the prayer of a righteous person powerful and effective?

There's no one correct answer to this question. You might talk about the fact that a righteous person (someone who is right with God because of their faith in Jesus) has a relationship with our all-powerful God who can do anything. You might talk about the idea that a righteous person prays in alignment with God's will.

**LEADING LESSONS
WEEK 5**

SAY

Let's talk more about the power and effective-ness of prayer. To do that, we need to look at the context (the surrounding verses) for James 5:16.

Read James 5:13-18.

What circumstances of life
does James mention?

How should we as Christians respond to
the circumstances of life?

What qualification does James add to how we should pray?

See verse 15. James mentions the "prayer offered in faith" (see also James 1:6

Why is faith important to how we pray?

More than anything else, God wants us to trust him. When we doubt (Jas. 1:6), we're saying we don't really believe God has the power to answer our prayers.

Elijah was a great leader and a prophet in Old Testament times. What do you learn about him and his prayer life?

Elijah is an example of an ordinary man who prayed faith-fully, and God responded in remarkable ways. We have the same power through faithful prayer that is in line with God's will.

LEADING LESSONS
WEEK 5

SAY

As mentioned earlier, James was one of Jesus' brothers. While he may not have been a full believer in Jesus until after Jesus arose from the dead, James must have learned a lot from Jesus over the years.

Throughout the Gospels, we see Jesus getting away from the crowds so that he could spend time alone with his heavenly Father in prayer. Luke 5:16 says, "Jesus often withdrew to lonely places and prayed." Jesus was the greatest leader who ever lived, so let's look at an example of how prayer was a part of Jesus' leadership.

Read Luke 6:12-19.

LEADING LESSONS
WEEK 5

What did Jesus do before he chose his apostles?

SAY

Jesus knew that the selection of these apostles was a huge decision. The future of his ministry, the church, and the spread of the gospel rested largely on whom he chose. So, rather than making this decision based solely on human wisdom, he spent the entire night in prayer. Now, consider this: Jesus was God's Son. He was in his very nature God, although he "did not consider equality with God something to be used to his own advantage" (Phil. 2:6). So, if Jesus needed to pray before making a decision, we do all the more!

What did Jesus do after he chose the apostles?

He went with them to where hurting people were. He taught and healed the people.

LEADING LESSONS
WEEK 5

SAY

This passage demonstrates how Jesus led. He always started by spending time communicating with his heavenly Father in prayer. Next he and his community (his disciples) would go together to where people were. Then finally they would minister to the people. The order of Jesus' leadership was: Prayer --- Community --- Ministry. It was never the other way around!

From what we've studied in James and Luke, what is the relationship between prayer and leadership?

LEADING LESSONS
WEEK 5

EVEN DEEPER

If you would like to dig even deeper into what the Bible says about prayer and leadership, look up and discuss the following Scripture passages. (Write these references in your Manhood Journey Notebooks.)

1 Kings 17:1; 18:41-46
Luke 22:39-46
Mark 1:35-39
Matthew 14:22-36
Colossians 4:2-6

SERVING
OTHERS

LEADING LESSONS 1 ON 1 GUIDE

SAY

Let's review some of the tips about prayer we discussed in our meeting:

Personal Prayer Tips

1. Prayer doesn't have to be out loud; it can be in the form of silent prayers through the day.

2. We must have our minds filled each day with God's Word and commune with him in prayer.

3. We can expect God to unleash power when we pray. Psalm 65:5 says, "You answer us with awesome deeds of righteousness, O God our Savior."

4. Each of us needs to find a regular time when we can pray one-on-one with God, and with others, especially with our family.

Leadership Prayer Tips

1. As a leader, you acquire the mind of God through prayer and the reading of the Word.

2. Then, when difficult decisions need to be made, you can draw on the wisdom of God in you.

3. If you try to lead without the mind of God, you'll tend to want to feed your own ego, and you'll think people need to do what you say just because you're the leader.

4. If you are constantly following God and hearing from him through prayer and the Word, you can be a more confident leader. The Holy Spirit will lead you as you lead others. Your decisions will be more in line with God's will and less about your own gain.

Before we go out to serve others or lead others, we must do as Jesus did and start with prayer.

With that in mind, what do you want to pray for?

Lead your son to discuss areas where he will be serving or leading others this week and then talk about how he (and you) can and will pray about that. Also, be sure to share with him the areas where you need to trust God in your service and leadership. Move naturally into a time of prayer.

TALKING
WITH GOD

LEADING LESSONS 1 ON 1 GUIDE

Prayer should come naturally out of your discussion. Use these prompts as needed:

LEADING LESSONS
WEEK 5

SAY

• You are our almighty God. We recognize your presence with us right now. We recognize your all-surpassing power. We pray for your purposes—for your will, not our own, to be done.

• Lord, we surrender our service and leadership to you.

• We trust you with your prayers.

• I need your help, Lord, this week as I _____ (how you will serve or lead).

• Everything we do, Father, wherever we serve or lead, we do it all for you, for your glory.

LEADING LESSONS
WEEK 5

LEADING LESSONS
WEEK 6

WHO WANTS TO LEAD?

A WORD TO DAD

Perhaps the best image of biblical leadership is that of a shepherd. God's Word is rich in its discussion about shepherding. Moses, David, and Amos served as shepherds, and all were influenced greatly by that role in their leadership. Shepherd is applied in Scripture to God, Jesus, kings and other political leaders, and ministers (not necessarily paid staff ministers).

As a dad, you shepherd your family (the sheep) in the following ways:

- *You feed the sheep even if you have to gather them in your arms to carry them to the pasture.*

- *You guide them to the pasture and away from the rough places and precipices.*

- *You seek and save any sheep who get lost.*

- *You protect the sheep; you are willing to sacrifice your own life for them.*

- *You restore sheep who go astray and return.*

- *You reward the sheep for obedience and faithfulness.*

- *You keep the sheep separate from the goats.*

But there's something incredibly important you must know about shepherd-leadership: You are actually an "undershepherd," not the shepherd of the sheep. The Bible indicates that

LEADING LESSONS
WEEK 6

there is one shepherd, and it's not you! Of course, it's referring to Jesus (John 10:16). He is the Good Shepherd (John 10:11, 15), the Great Shepherd (Heb. 13:20-21), and the Chief Shepherd (1 Peter 5:4). Your role is to follow the Chief Shepherd, model following him for your family, help the sheep under your care hear and respond to the Good Shepherd's voice, guide the sheep under your care to follow the Good Shepherd, reach out to sheep without a Shepherd, and lead the sheep to the Shepherd who gives abundant and eternal life.

BUILDING
OUR RELATIONSHIP

LEADING LESSONS 1 ON 1 GUIDE

GROUP SESSION REVIEW

Engage your son(s) in a dialogue about the meeting and the Leading Lessons module using any of the following questions:

LEADING LESSONS
WEEK 6

• How did you think the activity went in which a volunteer led the discussion of Psalm 23?

> How did he handle leading the discussion when the group was disruptive?

> How do you think the leader knew how to lead the discussion? (How has our regular, adult leader modeled leadership for us?)

• What did you learn about shepherds and sheep?

• From the other verses we read and discussed, what did you learn about shepherd-leadership?

• Let's review the Leading Lessons module so far (look back at your Manhood Journey Notebooks to help you recall your discussions):

> In Week 1, we discussed why leaders make rules. What do you remember from that session?

> In Week 2, we talked about how leaders are first of all followers of Christ. Why is that important?

> What were the three "P"s of leadership? (Power, Proverbs, and Prayer)

- Let's look back in our Manhood Journey Notebooks at the verses we've memorized during this module.

  › Which was your favorite. Why?

  › Which was the most difficult to memorize or live by? Why?

- What principle(s) of godly leadership stand out the most to you? Why?

LEADERSHIP DEFINED

SAY

Over the past six weeks, we've talked a lot about what godly leadership is and what it isn't. Yet, leadership is a broad topic that's hard to define in one simple sentence. Two leadership writers said that they discovered more than 850 different definitions of leadership!

LEADING LESSONS
WEEK 6

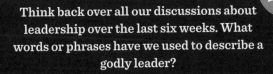

Think back over all our discussions about leadership over the last six weeks. What words or phrases have we used to describe a godly leader?

Flip through your Manhood Journey Notebooks to find these descriptions. Then write your list on a new page in your notebooks.

Here are some of the words you may find: love, obedience, follower (of Jesus), a person after God's heart, servant, humble, weak, dependent on God's power, under Jesus' authority, wise, pray-er, faithful, shepherd.

What other words of phrases have you heard that describe who a leader is?

You might come up with words such as "influencer," "persuader," "boss," or others.

LEADING LESSONS
WEEK 6

Let's come up with our own definition of a leader, based on these descriptions we've come up with. How would you fill in this blank?

A leader is _____.
(You can use more than one word.)

Write your definition in your Manhood Journey Notebooks.

SAY

Now let's look at one more important way that God's Word describes leadership, one we talked about in our meeting.

**LEADING LESSONS
WEEK 6**

KNOWING
GOD'S WORD

LEADING LESSONS 1 ON 1 GUIDE

THEME VERSE

"Be shepherds of God's flock that is under your care, watching over them —not because you must, but because you are willing, as God wants you to be."
1 Peter 5:2

For younger boys, use the following version or simply shorten the verse.

"Like shepherds, tend the flock of God among you. Watch over it. Don't shepherd because you must, but do it voluntarily for God"
1 Peter 5:2
(Common English Bible).

LEADING LESSONS
WEEK 6

Write this verse at the top of a new page in each of your Manhood Journey Notebooks and work on memorizing it.

DIGGING DEEPER

SAY

In our Bible study today, first we'll look at a negative example of shepherd-leadership, and then we'll investigate a positive one.

Ezekiel was priest who became a prophet of God during a very difficult time for God's people. The Israelites were being held captive by the mighty and evil Babylonians, and they were losing their identity as God's people. They refused to acknowledge or accept this tragic problem, and Ezekiel was called by God to change the people's minds and to come back to God. This is what a godly leader often must do. We are called by God to help people see that there really is a problem and then to guide them, teach them, and convince them to follow God.

In Chapter 34 of Ezekiel, the prophet was called by God to speak truth to the official religious leaders of Israel. In most Bible versions, these

SAY

leaders are called shepherds, because that's how God viewed his leaders. In The Message, they are called "shepherd-leaders." These shepherd leaders were not leading the people as God had called them to, which had caused much of the decline of the people's spiritual lives. Something had to be done!

As we read this passage, look at how God defines the role of a shepherd-leader.

TIPS

As you read through the passage, circle, underline, or highlight words or phrases on the pages of your Bibles that describe godly leadership. For instance, you might underline "take care of the flock" at the end of verse 2.

Yes, it is OK to write in your Bibles! While the Bible is God's Holy Word, the pages themselves are merely physical, perishable objects.

Read Ezekiel 34:1-10.

What words or phrases describe godly leadership?

Write these down in your Manhood Journey Notebooks.

What was the result of the leaders' failure to lead well? (see vv.5-6)

Who did the Israelite people, belong to?

See vv. 6, 8, 10. God calls them "my sheep" and "my flock."

LEADING LESSONS WEEK 6

What consequences were there for the leaders' failure to be good shepherds?

The key word is in verse 10: "accountable" ("responsible" in the NLT).

SAY

This is an important part of leadership! Here and in other places in the Bible we're told that when we become leaders, God holds us accountable for how we lead and what we teach (see Matt. 12:36; Rom. 14:12; 1 Cor. 4:2; Jas. 3:1). If we are to be godly leaders, we must be sure we lead in the way God is directing us through his Word and we must teach sound doctrine. We'll discuss this more as we look at the next passage in our Bibles.

Read 1 Peter 5:1-4.

LEADING LESSONS WEEK 6

Again, circle, underline, or highlight words or phrases that describe godly leadership. For instance, you might underline "shepherds" in verse 2.

SAY

An elder is a church leader, but the descriptions of leadership here apply to any kind of godly leader.

What words or phrases describe godly leadership?

Write these down in your Manhood Journey Notebooks. Some of the words and phrases you might discuss are: "shepherd," "willing," "as God wants you to be," "eager," "serve," and "examples." Also, don't miss "under your care" and "entrusted to you." You'll discuss those in a moment.

Why is it important for a leader to be "willing" and "eager"?

Why should a leader be "eager to serve"?

In the Ezekiel passage, we talked about accountability for leadership. What does this passage in 1 Peter say about accountability?

The answer may not be immediately obvious, so keep digging, looking especially at the phrases, "under your care" and "entrusted to you."

SAY

The people we lead are "entrusted to us" by God. He puts them under our care to love them, serve them, shepherd them, encourage them, and keep them safe from false teaching and other schemes of the devil. The people we lead belong to God. They are his creation and his children. We lead out of an act of "stewardship," that is, taking care of what actually belongs to God. That's a huge privilege and a great responsibility, but remember, God gives us the power and wisdom to lead well.

In the Ezekiel passage, we looked at the consequences for the leaders' poor shepherd-leadership. What are the rewards in 1 Peter 5 for good shepherd leadership? (See verse 4.)

LEADING LESSONS
WEEK 6

SAY

Jesus is ultimately our Chief Shepherd-Leader. When we follow him and lead his way, he'll reward us with more than we can even imagine!

EVEN DEEPER

If you would like to dig even deeper into what the Bible says about shepherd-leadership, look up and discuss the following Scripture passages. (Write these references in your Manhood Journey Notebooks.)

John 21:15-17
Proverbs 27:23
Acts 20:22-36
Hebrews 13
John 10:1-18

LEADING LESSONS
WEEK 6

SERVING
OTHERS

LEADING LESSONS 1 ON 1 GUIDE

After investigating leadership in this module, how willing and eager are you to serve by leading others?

What do you sense you need to do to continue to grow as a follower of Jesus and a godly leader?

SAY

Our involvement in Manhood Journey helps us grow as followers and as leaders. Our small group with other men and sons gives us accountability, support, and encouragement, which we need to keep growing to be more Christ-like.

LEADING LESSONS
WEEK 6

If you're part of a Manhood Journey small group, use this question:

Between now and when our group starts the next module, how do you want to continue moving forward? Do you want to keep meeting weekly or take a break?

Pull out the Module Map (available for purchase at www. manhoodjourney.org/module-map.) Or look at the descriptions of all the modules at www.manhoodjourney.org/modules. Talk about what other topics you would like to address in the future.

Who could we invite to join us in our next Manhood Journey small group?

Consider men and their sons from church; your son's friends from school, on a team, or in the neighborhood; or your friends, co-workers, or neighbors.

LEADING LESSONS
WEEK 6

If you are not in a Manhood Journey small group, use the following discussion points. Use the Module Map or look through the list of modules on the Manhood Journey website (www.manhoodjourney.org) as you discuss:

Which module do you want to work through next?

This could be a great opportunity to start our own Manhood Journey small group. What would you think about exploring that option?

TIPS

You'll find lots of resources and ideas for doing so on the Manhood Journey website under the "Get Started" tab.

LEADING LESSONS
WEEK 6

Close your time together in prayer, using any of the following prompts:

• Father, we recognize that you are present with us right now. Thank you for being near to us and desiring to spend time with us.

• We also recognize that you are our real Leader, our Chief Shepherd. You are all-powerful and all-knowing, and you are sovereign—you are in control of everything.

• Lord, as you call us to follow you and then to lead, please give us everything we need to lead well.

• We ask that you lead us in all of our next steps as we mature as followers, as we grow as shepherd-leaders, and as we decide what to do next in our Manhood Journey.

A FINAL WORD TO DAD

Borrow your son's Manhood Journey Notebook and then privately write another note to him on the next empty page. Tell him again how proud you are of him for completing this Leading Lessons module with you. Let him know that you look forward to spending more time together in pursuing godly manhood and godly leadership. Write a brief prayer for him, something like, "God, I thank you for my son, _____. I thank you for working powerfully in his life to help him become a more godly man, a more devoted follower of Jesus, and a growing leader. I know you will use him in incredible ways in the future as you lead him." Be sure to sign and date it.

Leave his notebook on his pillow before he goes to bed.

NOTE TO DAD FROM MEN OF MJ

God is using you in ways you probably can't see or even imagine! It's our prayer to God at Manhood Journey that out of his glorious riches he may strengthen you with power through his Spirit in your inner being, so that Christ may dwell in your heart through faith. And we pray that you, being rooted and established in love, may have power, together with all the Lord's holy people, to grasp how wide and long and high and deep is the love of Christ, and to know this love that surpasses knowledge—that you may be filled to the measure of all the fullness of God. Now to him who is able to do immeasurably more than all we ask or imagine, according to his power that is at work within us, to him be glory in the church and in Christ Jesus throughout all generations, for ever and ever! Amen (Ephesians 3:16-21).

CONTINUING A MANHOOD JOURNEY GROUP IS EASY

This kit contains everything you need to begin your journey, including:

• Embarking Group Guide - 6 week discussion on the five key areas of Biblical Manhood

• 1 on 1 Guide for daily actitives and study with your son(s)

• DVD of the introductory videos for the first 6 modules

• (10) Maprochures – an informational brochure/map of the first 6 modules

SAVE 20%
use coupon code: MJEN20

ALSO AVAILABLE

GROUP GUIDES

on 6 key topics of
biblical manhood

ON 1 GUIDES

or daily activities &
iscussion with your
on(s)

SHOP AT WWW.MANHOODJOURNEY.ORG